DEFENSELESS WATERS

Lu & Dick,

In celebration of poetry!!

love,
Francisca Jaleguche

MAY 2001

el ANDAR BOOKS

edited by Julia Reynolds

publisher Jorge Chino

DEFENSELESS WATERS

Francisca Valenzuela

illustrations by the author

el ANDAR BOOKS
Santa Cruz, California

El Andar Books is an imprint of El Andar Media Corporation

PO Box 7745

Santa Cruz, California 95061

(831) 457-8353   books@elandar.com

www.elandar.com

"Defenseless Waters"

1998, 1999, 2000

© Francisca Valenzuela

ISBN 0-9706978-0-5

Printed in the United States of America

10   9   8   7   6   5   4   3   2   1

CONTENTS

Introduction by Celia Correas Zapata

3	Silky Blue Butterfly	36	Michelle
5	The Tree	37	Star Songs
6	Tough Woman	38	Fear
7	Tea With Love	40	Lend My Heart
8	Dangle	41	Desert
9	Cedar	42	Tin Cup
10	Afterwards	44	Silhouette
11	Mistake	45	Sleep
12	Soul's Secret	46	Covet The Dead
13	We Roam	48	Gentleman
14	Strange World	51	Tranquil Sea
17	I Know It's Me	52	Weathered Stone
19	Las Vegas	53	Falling
20	Tune of Serenity	54	Woman
21	Happy	56	Childish System
23	Artist	57	Night of Mystery
24	Confusion	58	Palette of Paint
26	Weeping Willow	61	Mango Sap
27	Confessions From a Striped-Suited Mama	62	Emptiness
		63	Sailor
30	Doubtful Person	64	Polarized Mirror
31	Moment of Peace	65	Obsessed
32	I Come From Afar	66	Black Horizon
35	Defenseless Waters		

Introduction
by Celia Correas Zapata

These poems were written from mid-1998 to March of 1999. Francisca was living mostly in Berkeley, attending fifth grade at Park Day Elementary School, with occasional trips to Chile for long holidays and summer recess.

At this stage, however, her world is not centered geographically. The young poet appears to have embarked upon an inner journey towards a land of wonder, inhabited by magic creatures, presented with an eye for mood and color. In Silky Blue Butterfly, she says:

> Once I knew a butterfly
> who wore silky blue wings and
> two long antennas
>
> a crab who wore skin of fire
>
> a wolf who wore a coat of velvet

But a reflective mood takes over in Tough Woman, when confronted by poverty and helplessness, before the figure of a pregnant woman who has begotten four other children:

> She wears nothing but rags and dirty dresses, and
> lives in a home with nothing but walls
>
> and she thinks she´s so tough,
> even though I see the fear and worry hiding beyond the
> rough
> skin

Humorous introspection and contrasting views of appreciation and self deprecation contribute to a playful self-portrait in I Know it´s Me:

> My eyes are round and it seems as though
> born in spring, they´re meant for fall,
> and my hair is thick it should be for winter
> and my body thin should be for summer
>
> my love is deep but my
> affection is shallow

Awesome and strangely crafted, Covet the Dead, brings a Medieval apparition of a beautiful dead woman:

> Though you covet the dead
> figure
> frail, silent and grey
> two jade eyes
> piercing the porcelain
> skin and
> ropes of gold
> falling over the bare chest

Francisca´s poetry is surprising for any poet at any age.

DEFENSELESS WATERS

SILKY BLUE BUTTERFLY

Once I knew a butterfly
who wore silky blue wings and
two long antennas.
She was so attentive,
and beautiful and so pleasant.
And that butterfly,
knew a crab who wore skin of fire
and eight arms (or legs)
which walked him along the sandy shore.

He was very interesting
and charming.
And that crab,
knew a wolf
who wore a coat of velvet
which only the moon could make,
of silver and gray and eyes of pure wisdom,
light and mystical.
And that wolf howled at the moon,
with a cry so loud and so amazing,
a wolf so magical and a cry so wondrous
that only the stars could listen to his howl.
So every time I hear a wolf,
I think of the silky blue butterfly,
which had a friend who was a crab,
who had a friend which was a wolf.

THE TREE

The Tree's branches reach out to the sky as if
they were arms ready to fly me up to the heavens
where everything's right and that Tree
tells me I'm okay, even though I see little birdies around my head
and I'm in my bed with twinkling lights and
when I think about it the whole time through,
I think it's all The Tree's fault.

TOUGH WOMAN

I stare at the woman who bears
five children:
one baby,
one toddler,
one kid,
one older kid and
one teen though
carrying another bundle in her tummy.
Her dreams have faded into the background scenery
since she is now a housewife with no pay but pressure.
She wears nothing but rags and dirty dresses and
lives in a home with nothing but walls.
Her face is tired and smeared with perspiration.
Her arms are strong but weak and she is bold but
shy and she talks like a child
and she thinks she's so tough,
even though I see the fear and worry hiding beyond the rough
skin.

TEA WITH LOVE

love knocked on my door one day
i opened and she smiled
her cheeks were plump and red from the heat
she plopped down on the large cushion
her vivid life drained out
stubborn i asked her foolish questions
as she sipped in silence her tea
once in a while i would sneak a peek into the palms of her hands
and there i would see a red passion
a red fire cradled in her lovely warmth
she extended it to me and whispered
"your time has come dear"
i could only smile

DANGLE

My dreams have been caught in the dense air of
midnight,
and it seems it will be hard to retrieve them once more since
the wind has swallowed their silly pride,
their foolish ways.
I crawl over the coldest ground of dirt
as I appear
next to a phantom of dreams and fears
whose
face is covered in a clear
mask of hate.
Once I turn away toward the stairs I
find a little cave and it seems it's full of
shadows playing as I see
the walls with dancing silhouettes among the ashes of
the fire.
And I reach the door facing out toward the dark past
and the nearest future,
with the strongest wind hurling and prancing around me,
and there in the midnight sky,
misty and black,
I see my dream dangle.

CEDAR

Weave your roots into the
fertile ground
      thus you reach the
      sole of the earth.
Your veils of ice
           and flaring white
can swim beneath
the tightened air.
      Can you spin your arms in
a graceful dance like me?
      Can you sing a soft melody
so vibrant as mine?
Though you are beautiful
drenched in unlimited peace
      your body is no more
than a prickly trunk of
          wood
and your delicacy is no more than
      spears
      of
      green

AFTERWARDS

I savour what is only left of the quiet.
I possess what is only left of the passion.
I endear what is only left of the feeling.
I seize what is only left of you.

MISTAKE

I bend toward you and see in your face regret since they're
waiting for you
to be sent away and what can I say or do for you since it was
your mistake.
I take it when
your eyes are wet and you're not set to face the truth nor the real
youth you
spent and wasted,
though you tasted what it was like to lie,
to run,
and to be sent to die or something like that.

SOUL'S SECRET

I am standing in silence
and it seems I am trapped in myself
a shadow of what I used to be.
Buried in the pit of my soul
I planted secrets not to be revealed and
guilt which was not to be felt.

I stand in the presence of my own self and I stand
alone and bearing nothing but my own skin as
clothes all alone I stand
and I am ashamed but the beauty that is inside must
live on.

WE ROAM

We roam in a sky of thankful clouds
and a golden sun
which
bows its head at us
day after day
until
its rays are bruised with violet stains and
blue streaks.
When the moon appears
waiting to embrace
the pitch-black sky
and the diamonds
of twinkling wishes
that taunt
the clouds to come closer
drown in the winds of an icy taste
of snowflakes
the humid air haunts the skin of mine
under a streak of golden lightning
under a streak of pale white.

STRANGE WORLD

Savages wander through the gentle breeze
the ants attack the sensitive Giants and
without hesitation the mouse chases the cat
and the dog judges the fight with complete attention
while the Student instructs
the Teacher and the concerned child warns the parent not to
run off
when we live in a world which makes us afraid,
even though it could be worse.

I KNOW IT'S ME

I know my smile is not convincing,
or that I have to think twice about
wincing
when someone contemplates my
troubled self,
my unique form of being me,
I come around to see faces staring and looking.

My eyes are round and it seems as though
born in spring they're meant for fall,
and my hair is thick it should be for winter
and my body thin should be for summer.

My dreaming's high
but my hopes are low and
my relationships are awkward but my
friends are subtle and
my love is deep but my
affection is shallow.

So I glide upon the earth with
skinny legs and an overbite,
protruding ribs and
short fingernails but long
fingers to reach the
black and white keys on
my favorite instrument,
and throughout every detail,
I know it's me underneath everything.

LAS VEGAS

The thick smoke comes out from the cigarettes the
women
suck while arguing and coveting each other's luck
with men
or physical beauty when
down at the bar some men are fighting
while the others are lighting
pipes or drinking beer with extra ice.
Las Vegas.
Who knows what'll happen next.

TUNE OF SERENITY

I sucked my breath and
tucked in my chin as I walked
through the endless
        helplessness.
I passed a streetlight and caught myself staring
at a man with only saliva to quench his thirst
and crumbs
        to help his cravings too.
I walk straight but do not speak,
for scared I hum a tune of
        serenity
for only my ears to hear
to block away what I do not want to see.

HAPPY

The man stands alone, with no words to
his lips,
no motion except silence.
But
that smile spread across his face has nothing
to tell to any one,
except he is happy.

ARTIST

Flaunt the color of anger
        sketch images of hate
sculpt opaque figures to weld
        your emotion with reality.
Your posture is still and you
capture
a
moment
which you will make
        to live
                forever.

CONFUSION

 Singing without Notes
Talking without Voice
 Writing without Words
Voting without Choice
 Closing without Opening
Dying without being Born
 Watching without Seeing
Schools with nothing to Learn
 Evil without Good
Moon without Stars

Sun without Clouds
Perfection without Difference
 Sea without Waves
Fire without Flames
 Sweetness without Bitterness
Happiness without Tears
 Shame without Pride
Protection without Fear
 Guilt without Innocence
Love without Hate
 Darkness without Dawn
Destiny without Fate
 Hiding without Revealing
Life without Death
 Enemies without Friendships
Breathing without a Breath.

WEEPING WILLOW

Your tears are streaming down
leaking with green liquid
you are an ordinary willow
weeping alone.

CONFESSIONS FROM A STRIPED-SUITED MAMA

In striped suits
black and white
white and black

(the room was spinning out of control
while little Jessie was crying
as Gary scared the hell outta me
as he beat the baby
red the baby was a sea of red
as I grabbed the gun
[it was so close!]
one pull and it would stop
all of it would stop
stop
you know what it's like for somethin' to stop?

I know it was wrong
but I was defending myself
defending Jessie
couldn't they see Gary was gonna kill him if I didn't do it?)

They work while beads of sweaty perspiration
dance on their foreheads
and glimmer on their necks
they reminisce about their fractured hearts their bruised souls
contemplating the rich life that they will not live
absorbing the fresh air while it lasts

(you know what it's like in this dump?
it's dark a waste of time a waste of dignity a waste of humanity
it's foul and dingy
and dirty

overflowing like a sour sea with fishes dead fishes
wasted skin that just breathes cause there's no soul in there
[it was lost long ago]
like murderers
and hookers
and thieves
and women defending their babies: hey that's me?!

I know it was wrong
and I get I was crazy
but them girls in here
they sell their bodies
for dope and crack and shit like that
in the slammer they have connections with the outside [maybe inside, too]
but
SHHHHHHHH
the cops don't know it yet)

DOUBTFUL PERSON

I
always doubt whether my decision
is efficient
doubt if i would be better off
as another person
doubt if
my surroundings my environment my life
can shatter like a thin crystal glass
absorbed by doubt i wonder
if i'm as good as i can be
if i can be better

i'm becoming too much of a doubtful person.

MOMENT OF PEACE

I return but am forgiven
for the sins I'm bound to bear
are crawling up my hopes and
wishes but I hush them so
I will at least have a moment of peace.

I COME FROM AFAR

I come from afar;
where hills of gold stretch beyond
a
marble sea
　　　　of ivory waves and glass pearls of black.
'Tis where
grains of silver
caress our skin
and
crystalline waters
wash our bodies.
I come from afar
where justice
　　　　is fair
where life is so simple
as one's life should be.

DEFENSELESS WATERS

I coast upon a layer of thin ice,
its shallow waters are deep of affection
though the vacancy of hope is a misfortune
since the eagles fly over the defenseless waters,
which are now coming to ruins
with only weary waves and hollow shells of no heart
since it has frozen me and everything else.

MICHELLE

we used to sit talk play watch walk
together
now I ask her if she wants to play
"no time for that"
but she has time to flirt and squirm around
        with Mike
        with John
        with Mitchell
        with Tom
but she has time to puff cigarette butts and choke on them
since she knows they'll kill her
but she has time to stain her eyelids with blue and red and green
but she has time to absorb disgusting comments that men place on her ears
she has time to sniff to suck to snort to slit
I don't know what happened.

STAR SONGS

Quietly.

Look deeply.

Because if you do

The stars might sing a song for you.

FEAR

    The coat of delicacy shrivels up
        so you plummet down
            from
    so high above your status
        while the cackle of
            your shadow
    slices through black stars
        and now they leak ivory
        blood.

Your shadow,
  tantalizing
      intriguing and thickly
          twined with chivalry.
    Your own reflection,
stronger than you...
     How can that be?
It tortures and tickles
your pale face flushed
with envy.
    Fear trickles
down your back
    while you stand
on the pivot of your
        shadow.

LEND MY HEART

It has been too long
        to aspire to love.
For only I have slept
underneath the filthy sheets
in the unmade bed.
Reluctant I am
        to reach out once more;
it is an elusive thought
to lend my heart
        to another.

DESERT

Dry and alone it lives with no lives.
It hides the tourists.
It ignores the people.
Once in the day it will burst with
excitement throwing explosions
of hot yellow sand.
The desert will sit on its own.

TIN CUP

there may be a boy
crying
   begging
aching on the highway

a boy

a brother
a son
a nephew

a boy

but you and me
and them and us
will simply keep on driving
(why does the road seem so long?)

will change the radio
(why does the music seem so loud?)

will stare at
    our clean fingernails
(his are filthy city-stained fingernails)
with guilt

I know it's unfair but I don't stop to kneel over and
    help
to drop a penny a precious copper penny into the
    faded tin cup
sacrificing a little energy a little time a little dough
'cause I have you have we have
red Toyotas
food in our tummies and more in the wastebasket
in the fridge
    and worry if we'll get to see the new flick and
whether Jimmy'll invite us to the prom

and he worries
about what he will eat for dinner
whether or not
he will eat for dinner

SILHOUETTE

I nourish only your silhouette
for your soul objects to my devotion
as I blend into the crowds
        as another face
                as another burden.
For your possession is of another,
for your melody is heard by one other,
        and I feed you only tunes
     that your silhouette can dance to.

SLEEP

Restless you might turn and
twist,
nothing will help you
melt into the thickness of
the cotton sheets and
wool covers
with the aroma of your skin.
Shadows bounce from wall to wall by
the window where
the trees have contests to see
who is the strongest.
Slowly the visions of dreams come to sight.
The thick layers of starchy brown hair
over the purple linen,
eyes close...
Deep sleep.

COVET THE DEAD

    You delicately fold the
           remains of silk
    for if too rough you would
           obliterate
    the heavy pieces of coiled body.
    Though you covet the dead
           figure
    frail, silent and grey
           two jade eyes

piercing the porcelain
skin and
        ropes of gold
falling over the bare
chest which was observed
so carefully by the
eyes of so many.
        But no more shall
she be coveted
        but no more shall
she be observed
        for long gone she
floats above and rests
her fragile body
        over the icy waves
of sea.

GENTLEMAN

Humble and kind gentleman,
    would you care to do
        the
honors?
    For charming and handsome
you deliver an overwhelming
    aura of confidence
        and seduction.
    You
    coax us with enticing melodies
        while
    imprudently revealing
        gestures and

stares of no respect.
      You are
selfish and woven
        with pride.
So we see nothing but a
      pair of
insignificant eyes
       which try to
            weave
      volumes of love
         but only
              reach
the point of a despicable
        ugly
         demeanor

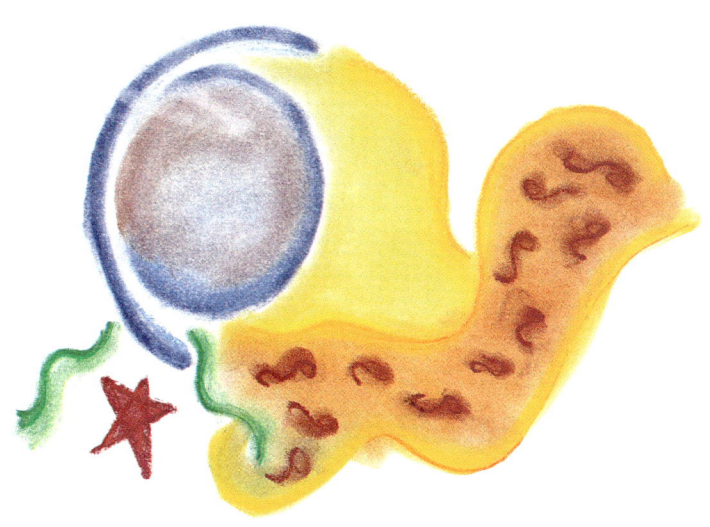

TRANQUIL SEA

We roll on a tranquil sea of
wild waves and
colorful fishes which wander
at the bottom of a sand castle
hiding underneath
strands of green or purple or
blue as
the sharks lurk in the rocky bottom
hunting for prey
so they won't go hungry and the
tide pools are overflowing with
clams and
we find glittering shells and small snails
and we sit and watch
the many different worlds all hidden under
the clear liquid
living their daily life
under the biggest sky of waves.

WEATHERED STONE

I stumble upon the
face of a
      weathered stone
tarnished by time
wasted by souls
soaked in ash it tells
      ancient legends
of times before
      yet not
when ignorance seeped
through one's eyes
      yet not
when hatred burned
through one's flesh
      penetrating so deep
one bleeds
wise that stone is,
weathered and old
      masked in ash it is,
grey and cold.

FALLING

I fall into the heavy guilt which weaves
a path to the beginning and
once more I rejoice but my voice is
caught and a hand is choking me too hard
and my
lips won't move with a cry and wail.
With a thrust and a hit I pull away but once more
I am tangled and I dangle
from the rooftops with shame and I fall over a river of
empty dreams which loosen their thoughts as
the current pushes them softly and
the hollow echo of voices from so long back makes faint
sounds in the background as I fall into a hole
in the ground as
everything gets blurry,
nothing is clear...
as I fall into myself once more.

WOMAN

I am a woman.
Powerful, strong and courageous.
I stand with pride, tall and graceful.
I hold the swan's delicacy,
The panther's passion,
The rose's beauty and the
Man's hard work.
Do not push me down, or stand in my way,
or I will crush you.
Do not tie me down with chains or splintered
Ropes.
For they will only sprain and burn,

But nothing else.

They cannot tie down my desire to be a free Woman,

Or my independence to work as a free human.

I can stand against anything,

Except fate.

I can crush anything,

Except love.

I can hurt anyone,

Except God.

I am a woman,

And can shine like the sun.

CHILDISH SYSTEM

it seems to me
that adults are just children
 of older age
that disguise their actions
in sophisticated words
long phrases that make it seem
that they are wiser
and it seems to me
that children are just like adults
  of younger age
that capture the simplicity of life:
the ripe breezes
the crystalline drops of morning dew on the tree leaves
the midnight shadows that dance on their skin
so it seems to me
that this system is absolutely perfect.

NIGHT OF MYSTERY

Bathed in the pale glow of silver
from the heavenly moon
onto a pool of black stillness;

a breeze may blow
a snake may hiss
but this is the night of mystery.

Lapping waves of drowning darkness
pound against shore.
Sand of prickly stones and shells
swim and dance under the white shine.

Slowly as the night grows deeper,
the lights of the stars dimmer,
when the time of wolves and owls come,
the mystery can now unfold.

PALETTE OF PAINT

Nude

folded and crumpled

smeared with scarlet

streaked with black

a palette of colors endured by her.

The satisfaction of throwing stones at her

is real.

Though out of proportion

and weak you stand

and you cast

paint of blue

to hurt and bruise

to point out your strength.

MANGO SAP

my withering soul melts
into the pool
of ripe shade
into the puddle
of bitter dandelion blood
into the pond
of sweet eager youth
as I sit and sip
mango sap

EMPTINESS

An untouched coffee mug sits patiently
on the kitchen counter
next to the wrinkled newspaper opened to the headline
page
even though no one is there to read it.
Eggs are boiled,
and the toast is burnt and
the refrigerator stands wide open
where a child had reached to get a soda
though Mom or Dad denied it.
The solitary rooms are empty and dark,
even though the windows are opened
and the sun shines in.
This house may stand all solemn,
but this house has kept itself solid within these
peeling yellow walls.
As the wind blows through the wasted
tired screen
creaking softly in the tune of
lovers and
a family.

SAILOR

Once again up on deck
he waves his arms
        once again he caresses the sea.
The boat sees its mission there
        laid out and stretched before it,
scattered in delicate pieces throughout the sky;
it slices the water and ripples the surface
                wrinkling the skin with creases of an old
                man's face.
Marveling at his creation, his boat—-
dancing on the silver fingertips of the sea,
the crystalline water slashing noisily around him
        he ponders
        his life is a fragile bubble of pure perfection
nobody could steal the feeling embracing him when he kissed the
        clouds
and thundered through the
                damp
salty, smell cradling his sea.
People just view him and perplexed they walk away.
He,
a simple sailor had a life nobody could buy.

POLARIZED MIRROR

it was like having a glass wall
one of those polarized mirrors, ya know?
they would laugh and joke and poke at each other
not sensing not seeing
that I existed
they would keep on chattering like chickens
they would keep on squawking like sea gulls
commenting, teasing, whining, complaining
until I stood up and left
        they were silent for a few minutes
wrapped in tense guilt, I hope
since soon they were up and at it again.

OBSESSED

I've memorized everything
the way you breathe
the way you speak
the way you watched me watching you
I've fallen in the depths of your being
all I wish is to be tangled with your soul
for you to explore my complexity
for you to intrude discover and later
most likely reject
I've become obsessed.
Obsessed.
        Obsessed.
Obsessed.

BLACK HORIZON

Soaked in ink
black piper
drunk with dark wine
and light desire
you are dressed in the shadows
wrapped in the night
in a coat of a million stars
and black velvet
which burns your flesh like
blue flames of fires
that ache beneath the skin of
midnight
and
the sun follows your dance of grace
when you awake
over the black horizon.

Designer: Johan De Meulenaere
Text: Janson Text 9.5/16
Display Type: Century Gothic 11 pt.
Printer: Erich Printing, San José, California